Writings on the Art
of the Book

The Book Maker's D e s i r e
Buzz Spector

Umbrella Editions 1995

*To Maria and Steve,
for all past and future
pages — Buzz Spector*

24 January 1996

© 1995 by Umbrella Associates
Published in the
United States of America

Umbrella Editions
P.O.B. 40100
Pasadena, CA 91114

Design:
Nan Goggin

Cover:
Buzz Spector,
History of Europe, 1983
Plaster over found book,
10 $^1/_2$ x 12 x 15 inches.

Photograph:
Chester Brummel, ©1995,
The Art Institute of Chicago,
All rights reserved.

ISBN: 0-9635042-1-5

Table of Contents

Introduction

Topics

7 Going Over the Books (1987)

11 Art Readings (1988)

15 The Fetishism of the Book Object (1991)

23 Buzz Spector: an interview with
Neva Lindburg Muñoz (1994)

Artists

31 Chambered Volumes: the book constructions
of Margaret Wharton (1987)

35 The Tome, The Tomb:
On Broodthaers (1987)

39 The Departure of the Argonaut (1987)

41 Anselm Kiefer's Bookworks (1989)

49 Baldessari's *Shandy* (1989)

53 Biblioselfconsciousness:
Walter Hamady's *Gabberjabs* (1991)

57 Byron Clercx: Reading Things (1993)

61 Residual Readings:
the altered books of Ann Hamilton (1995)

Caprices

67 Hair and Beets (1989)

69 A Letter to Anne Rorimer
about Marcel Broodthaers (1989)

73 Touching, Turning, and Yearning (1990)

76 Vertigo (1990)

77 Some Family Photographs (1994)

The closure of the book is an illusion largely created by its materiality, its cover. Once the book is considered on the plane of its significance, it threatens infinity. **Introduction**

You'll see here that I like reading, and indeed, this volume offers as much in reflection on that activity as on the critical circumstances of artists' books and book objects. As Susan Stewart has noted, "The closure of the book is an illusion largely created by its materiality, its cover. Once the book is considered on the plane of its significance, it threatens infinity." I'm also a materialist, and the analyses I apply to specific bookworks proceed from a concern with the relationship between their physical substance and the concepts articulated through their words and/or images.

For this collection, nearly all of the previously published essays and reviews have been reworked to some extent. In some cases I have virtually rewritten the entire document. A couple of these texts include material I excerpted from my own earlier writing, and I apologize for these redundancies.

This book wouldn't have seen print without the encouragement and persistence of Judith Hoffberg. Her support of the genre of artists' books arises from the most generous of passions. I am also grateful to Johanna Drucker, Joan Lyons, and Clive Phillpot, whose writing on artists' books has informed many of the views I am propounding here. My thanks to the various institutions who commissioned the catalogue essays, the journals and magazines who published the reviews, and to the artists whose works are so inspiring. Thanks, too, to Nan Goggin, who gave form to these pages in the extra hours she found who knows where. Finally, I want to thank my family for the fortitude they've demonstrated over the past year.

Buzz Spector
March 1995

Topics

Going Over the Books

I write this, by way of introduction, on the front porch of a small, green-painted clapboard cottage in the woods near Saugatuck, Michigan. My cottage has a name, "Mary Kay." It is within sight, through trees and underbrush, of two other cottages, "Scanlan" and "Duncan Clark," on the grounds of OxBow, the artists' colony on Lake Michigan's eastern shore. Out of sight, but faintly audible, are a number of artists blowing glass and making prints. There are painters here too, but theirs is a silent art. Others are reading books, or writing in them, also silent activities, being done here in part at my behest. I am visiting for a week to lead a workshop entitled "Book Concepts," whose ostensible purpose is to "focus on the production and critique of sequentially developed ideas and explore both traditional and nontraditional formats of the book." I take pleasure in fortuitous circumstance, and the coincidence of the workshop and an invitation from the editor of *Dialogue* to write a series of columns on the nature of artists' books, art books, and the culture of the book, seems most fortunate now.

This morning twelve of us met in the living room of the "Scanlan" to share observations, insights, and perturbations in the reading of a story by Jorge Luis Borges, "The Library of Babel." It is a narrative history of a world which exists somewhere in the form of a Library. All possible combinations of the letters of the alphabet are contained in the books on its shelves, and in the course of their wanderings through its galleries, the inhabitants of this library/world have come to know that no duplicate volumes exist in all its vast reaches.

Of particular interest to the members of the workshop was a

rumination by Borges' Librarian on the impossibility of an absolute compendium, an explanation of "the origin of the Library and of time." Even if the words to such a definition could be found, the question would still remain as to whether the awesome sentences were in the vocabulary of the reader or in another vocabulary assigning the same words different values. This melancholic reflection concludes with a parenthetical question: "You who read me, are you sure you understand my language?"

Borges standardized the books of his Babel so that their inconceivable uniformity would allow the equally inconceivable variety of the letters and words they contained to be seen. In their fictive status as containers for texts, they are made of insubstantial stuff. Borges understood the large problem the book as object posed for his evocation of the totality of language. He alludes to this in a footnote that reads in part: "no book is also a stairway, though doubtless there are books that discuss and deny and demonstrate this possibility and others whose structure corresponds to that of a stairway." The book Borges had in mind here is the familiar, conventional volume of so many pages, with such and such binding and a meticulous order of typographic characters in service to the author's words–characters effectively invisible as we scan them to make the text voice hearable in our minds.

The language of the book–as distinct from the words comprising its text–is one of pages, their density and heft; of covers, in cloth over boards or in paper; and of signatures (suites of pages created by folding large sheets of printed paper, later trimmed) sewn together within the protective curve of the spine, or cut in perfect alignment and then bound with glue. Some objects called books possess none of these things. Some have no words either, showing images instead–or not even images. In all these parts, as well as in the forms of the letters and methods of their placement upon the spread pages, the elements of a syntax are present.

Furthermore, and especially with artists of the book, these elements clearly constitute a style, not like that of the author, but"rather like the "vocabulary" of a painter or the "syntax" of a sculptor.

The generic book confronts us with its amalgamation of picture plane and sculptural volume. Its modest scale–in comparison with that of the generic painting or generic sculpture–implies modest claims upon our attention. Modesty, though, is a matter of appearances. We hardly know a book by looking at it, and when we truly "know" it, the knowing is engaged and intimate–a ravishment.

There is a growing critical interest in the role of the spectator with regard to visual art of the present or recent past. The nature of the gaze, the position of the observer as implied by the presentation of the work of art, the social and political aspects of the point-of-view; these are issues entailed in the (necessarily) public encounter between viewer and object in the gallery (or the gallery's stand-in).

But how unlike the gaze of a viewer is the attention paid by a reader to a book. Two aspects of this difference in cognizance are worth reflecting on here: its siting and its duration. Pausing before a picture in a gallery, we approach or retreat to find an optimum viewing distance. Encountering a three-dimensional work, we move around it, and this orbit has its apogee and perigee. The intention of any "site specific" work is to limit the viewer's choices of point-of-view. The purpose of anamorphic art is to invest the proper site of observation with a special, localized, representational reward. But all artworks share an attribute of site when installed for viewing. They are ready for a standing, public address by the people who come upon them. We dress up and go out to look at art. Undressed, in bed, we read.

The customary privacy of reading leads to unself-conscious absorption. One does not read as a pose (although posing as a reader is a common strategy). The space of reading is intimate: only the beloved's body comes closer to that of the reader than the book, held in the hands, resting on the chest, or nested in the lap.

Reading as an endeavor takes real time, as the textual or pictorial narrative develops through many turnings of pages. Books share this quality of real time with film and video. Their structural parceling of information enforces a duration of attention, a period of time which can be postponed or quickly consumed, at the volition of the reader.

Reading, with the physical interaction and luxurious duration that characterize it as an activity, evokes another order of significance, a seriousness of purpose, a seeking after truth, which the depiction of reading itself represents. Artists working with the form of the book are quite consciously attempting to solicit for their own endeavors the kind of attention ordinarily paid by readers to a text. The memory of reading infuses our manipulations of even the most drastically altered variants of the conventional book.

Previously published in **Dialogue**, *Volume 10, no. 5, September/October 1987.*

Art Readings

A pair of exhibits at the Chicago Public Library Cultural Center serve as cautionary examples of the ways language can be used and abused in works of art. Most of the items making up "Urgent Messages" and "Artists' Books–Illinois" are full of words; appropriately enough since the works are displayed in two galleries housed in a library building. That neither exhibit manages to provide a consistently effective verbal-visual dialectic says a lot about the frail coherence of words and pictures together, especially when mediums are given precedence over messages.

"Urgent Messages" is the larger of these two group surveys, both in terms of its conceptual and formal range and the geographic region from which its 53 midwestern and southern participants have been selected. Even so, it is surprising to realize that the paintings, sculpture, prints, and photographs displayed in the Cultural Center's fourth floor Exhibit Hall have more in the way of text than many of the bookworks mounted in plexiglass cases in the Randolph Gallery downstairs. Not that a text is essential to a book, of course. "Artists' Books–Illinois" focuses on the form of the book, not its conventional content. Still, a book is where we go looking for a story, and although you can, really, tell a lot about a book by looking at its form, a volume locked in a case is going to provide an unsatisfactory reading experience.

Don Baum, guest curator of "Urgent Messages," draws a distinction between the "intuitive, personal, diaristic, and autobiographical" language that characterizes the artists he has chosen, and those artists "pursuing a strictly formalistic conceptual approach." Baum names no names here, but this message-laden installation contains almost no work reminiscent of Robert Barry, Joseph Kosuth, or Lawrence Weiner. Neither is there much in the way of appropriated or critical language, as used by Victor Burgin, Jenny Holzer, or Barbara Kruger. There are quite a few works by naive artists, including Mary Bell, Reverend Howard Finster, Jesse Howard, Albert "Kid" Mertz, and Sister Gertrude Morgan, who are in every case far older (Bell, Howard, and Morgan are dead) than the academically trained artists that make up the rest of this selection. In this context the naives begin to assume the status of progenitors for the idiosyncratic words and narratives of their juniors.

Indeed, the naives seem to have more "urgency" in their messages than can be found anywhere else here, and some of the most effective, and affecting, mainstream works in the exhibition make obvious reference to their signboard style. David Dunlap's room-size installation, *Dreaming, He is at Work*, 1987, combines placards, shelves holding notebooks, words on the wall, and assorted artifacts in a sort of monumental diary and shrine to the memory of the Rev. Martin Luther King, Salvadoran Archbishop Oscar Romero, and other martyrs to the cause of social justice. The richly autobiographical and political references are psychologically enhanced by Dunlap's apparently naive methods of execution.

Timothy Jay Tobin's *Christ Image Tank, Fostoria, Ohio, Aug. '86*, 1987, is an altar-like construction with photos, newspaper clippings, and other paper ephemera pasted to the glass panes of a battered old farmhouse window hung between lintel posts. The collaged words and pictures are concerned with an apparition of Christ that some people saw on the side of an oil storage tank in Fostoria. The work suggests a window display by some rural evangelist. Nicole Ferentz's crudely constructed signboards are also formally reminiscent of naive art, but the jejune sophistication of their texts ("I tried to be nice," "They expected something different") is simply more of the ironic banality of so much of the contemporary image/text work seen here. Arch urban witticisms, psychobabble, disaffected reflections on the nature of art or identity, have all become clichés of language in artworks. It is somewhat as if these fragmented words and phrases drifted too far away from meaning and got trapped on the picture plane.

"Artists' Books–Illinois" includes works by 23 artists, three of whom–Sally Alatalo, Miles DeCoster, and Barb Van Tuyle–have submitted books that are displayed as such. That is, viewers can touch them and turn their pages. The remaining objects on display are framed or otherwise encased. The dilemma in staging exhibitions of books as art objects is the denial of access to the work that conservation necessarily demands. Any book that, by virtue of its uniqueness or fragility of materials, would be damaged by handling must be protected, even at the cost of intelligibility. This might have been a greater problem for the installation if more works on view needed to be read.

"Artists' book," as a term describing the form and function of the vanguard paginated work of the '60s and '70s, seems barely applicable to more than half of these objects. Most of the exhibit is comprised of beautifully printed and assembled volumes reflecting the increasingly retrograde fetishization of the book form. In several cases, the only explicable relationship between form and text is found in the structural pun connecting a particular literary allusion to the appearance of the object. The display that protects the works also exacerbates the difficulty in reading them, and it is a more than passing irony that implications of hermeticism and elitism should surround books shown to a public using the library as a means of gaining access to texts.

*Previously published in **Dialogue**, Volume 11, no. 1, January-February 1988.*

Dieter Roth, *Sammlung flachen Abfalls,*
(Collection of Flat Waste) 1982
photo: Museum of Contemporary Art, Chicago

The Fetishism of the Book Object

The unique book, also called "book object," is a genre of artwork that refers to the forms, relations, and configurations of the book. The history of this practise, and its several meanings, is informed by the histories of manuscripts and printed books, but the technological evolution of the codex form is of less importance in knowing the book object than is the reading these objects simultaneously solicit and refute.

Multiplicity is the very nature of the book. It is the theater of language, where writing is dressed up to perform. And also like theater, the textual performances of a book are enacted over and over again. Regardless of its linguistic graces, the utility of the book is a function of its numbers, circulating among legions of readers. For all its graphic or structural variety, the conventional book operates because its language is public and can be shared. It is precisely the "uniqueness" of the book object that redefines it in terms of art. This singularity, however, does not return the text of such a book to the status of manuscript. To be seen, singly, is the destiny of the book object; hence its language is superficial, an attribute among other attributes, lubricating the gaze of the viewer who, reading its words, responds instead to the codifications of its form.

When Stéphane Mallarmé described the folded and uncut signatures of books as "virginal,"[1] awaiting the penetration of the "paper knife," he identified an erotics of reading that some contemporary critics have characterized in more obviously sexual terms. For example, Susan Grubar has noted: "A 'passage' of a text is a way of knowing a 'corpus' or 'body' of material that should lead us on, tease us—but not too obviously. 'Knowing' a book is not unlike sexual knowing... Not only do we experience gratification orally as we 'devour' books voraciously, we also respond subliminally to the 'rhythms' of the plot, looking forward to a 'climax.'"[2]

Similarly, Roland Barthes offers a profile of the text as "a diagrammatic and not an imitative structure, [that] can reveal itself in the form of a body, split into fetish objects, into erotic sites."[3] Central to Barthes' reference is his identification of fetishism, the eroticized symbolmaking activity, with the conceptual engagement of reader and text. But the book object can also operate as a fetish, playing a part that stands in for a whole.

The topography of an open book is explicit in its erotic associations: sumptuous twin paper curves that meet in a recessed seam. Page turning is a series of gentle, sweeping gestures, like the brush of fingers on a naked back. Indeed, the behavior of readers has more in common with the play of intimacy than with the public decorum of art viewing or music listening. Most of us read lying down or seated and most of us read at least partially unclothed. We dress up to go out and look at art; undressed, in bed, we read. We seek greater comfort while reading than the furnishings of museums or concert halls will ever grant us. When we read—the conventional distance between eye and page is around fourteen inches —we often become the lectern that receives the book: chest, arms, lap, or thighs. This proximity is the territory of embrace, of possession; not to be entered without permission.

There are two primary ways to make a book object; constructing some singular variant of the book form, and altering a single copy of a found volume. The former method is allied to such domestic narrative projects as the scrapbook or photographic album, in which a collage of souvenirs evokes memories of past experience. Susan Stewart points to the discontinuity between the material survivals of such books and their referents: "Only the act of memory constitutes their resemblance. And it is in this gap between resemblance and identity that nostalgic desire arises. The nostalgic is enamored of distance, not of the referent itself."[4]

This distance also characterizes the relationship of the fetishist to the object of desire, in which possession simultaneously makes the object's status as substitution into an experience of loss and of a surplus of signification. The singularity of the unique book exaggerates the significance of the methods and materials of its making, even as it privatizes the experience of its possessor. As Stewart reminds us, "The further the object is removed from its use value, the more abstract it becomes and the more multivocal is its referentiality."[5] But unlike the fetish, whose value is independent of its intrinsic qualities or context of origin, the artist's intentions for the book object—the conditions of its display and classification—can serve to mediate the scenarios of fetishism.

The series of hardbound notebooks comprising Dieter Roth's *Sammlung flachen Abfalls* (Collection of Flat Waste), 1982, are filled with plastic sleeves containing every piece of flat material detritus the artist encountered over the period of a week. The thirty-one volume set parodies the fetishist collection through its inclusion of such vulgarities as soiled toilet paper and sodden cigarette butts. One could suppose that the collector who purchased the work might implicate these residues in transcendent reveries, but in fact the rigor of Roth's classification system redeems the work's materials for the purposes of the artist, that of engaging daily life in all its multitudinous qualities.

Anselm Kiefer's book objects are more concerned with the intersection of historical and physical processes. The cracked and dusty grit encrusting the covers and portions of the interior of *Märkischer Sand* V (March Sand V), 1977, literally crumbles as its pages of photographs covered with sand are turned, a phenomenal effect quite in line with the meaning of its pictorial narrative. The book's title joins allusions to a German Army marching song and the name of a scenic park southeast of Berlin, but the images of croplands and gently rolling hills are actually taken from the agricultural region surrounding Hornbach, near Buchen.

At the beginning of *Märkischer Sand V*'s sequence of twenty-five double page spreads, the photographs of wheatfields and scattered buildings convey a sense of generic plenitude. These images, alternating between details of stalks of grain and views of distant hills, are at first only lightly streaked with particles of sand in glue. These smears become more extensive as each page is turned until, in the book's final spreads, the photographs are completely buried under layers of sand and stones. Time passes here very eloquently and physically because with each turning page the reader awakens the work through the sloughing off of its substance.

A number of artists have altered found books, transforming their conventional form into tableaus (by painting, piercing, or studding the covers so as to "fix" the book in the open or closed position), containers (by excising or imbricating the text block), or topographies (by pasting over and/or tinting pages so as to overlay the text with a visual metanarrative). This kind of work uses the found book as an armature from which to operate, changing our relationship to the object from reader to viewer while simultaneously shifting our orientation from the visual to the tactile. Dependent on our recognition of its previous identity, the altered book is fundamentally allegorical, its (text) body a "ruin" that is supplemented by an overabundance of material effects.

The altered book can also be traced to that crucial modernist paradigm, the "readymade." In fact, Marcel Duchamp's *Unhappy Readymade*, 1919, was a geometry textbook hung out on a Paris balcony until it was destroyed by the wind and rain. Duchamp described the work in an interview with Pierre Cabanne: "...the wind had to go through the book, choose its own problems, turn and tear out the pages....It amused me to bring the idea of happy and unhappy into readymades, and then the rain, the wind, the pages flying, it was an amusing idea..."[6]

Duchamp's book, unhappy with its dissolution, is merely one copy among copies. It has been singled out only by the context of its destruction. But *Unhappy Readymade* is different from Duchamp's other chosen objects in that the book selected for this readymade had an author. The "documentation" of this readymade consists of a single fuzzy photograph and a small oil painting, executed by Duchamp's sister, Suzanne. From this record it is impossible to identify the specific edition chosen for the work. The book's employment as a generic exemplar was intended to overwhelm the specific text of the unknown geometrician contained within its covers, but it succeeds in that endeavor only through a lack of disclosure that operates quite differently from the given anonymity of whoever made the bicycle wheel, snow shovel, or urinal.

In the case of Marcel Broodthaers' *Pense Bête*, 1964, the artist interred the unsold copies of his last book of poems in a base of crudely modeled plaster. Benjamin H.D. Buchloh has called this the "very first work" of Broodthaers' *oeuvre*, "which terminated his failure as a poet and began his career as an artist."[7] Dieter Schwarz subsequently differentiated Broodthaers' gesture from the operations of the readymade:
"In contradistinction to the readymade, which is selected by its 'author,' being thereby instated as an aesthetic object, the poems of *Pense Bête* remain part of literary discourse, for the author's 'statement' is obviously, by its means of presentation (book and typography), inscribed within an existing cultural tradition."[8]

Yet, Broodthaers is twice the author here, and the primacy that

Buchloh assigns to the art gesture simply reflects his understanding of its concrete effect. Both Buchloh and Schwarz cite a later interview in which Broodthaers expressed surprise that his gesture of interdiction didn't arouse the curiosity of his viewers:

"Here you cannot read the book without destroying its plastic qualities. I believed that this concrete gesture would have confronted the viewer with this interdiction. But very much to my surprise the viewer reacted in a totally different manner than I had expected.... Nobody was curious to read the text, not knowing whether they were looking at interred prose, or poetry, sad or pleasant. Nobody was affected by the interdiction."[9]

Broodthaers was undoubtedly speaking ironically, since his casting gesture removed that text from the interpretive schema by which his books themselves were understood as a collection of fragments.

Clive Phillpot has decried the atavistic tendencies of book objects, noting that they "celebrate only bookishness, but deny the book's function," and concluding that "the fetishization of the form of the book may also be an antiliterate gesture, an escape into the image of this demanding medium."[10]

This criticism seems particularly applicable to the excisions, erasures, immolations, and other text obliterating methods of altering found books. But these transformations of text to work take place in the shadow of the subject book's publication. The elegiac sensibility that infuses so many alterations of conventional books gains some portion of its resonance from the inherent futility of such singular transformations considered against the ubiquity of the edition. The book is always partial; hence always susceptible to the alienating labor of the fetish. Only the text is total.

A shorter version of this essay, entitled "The Book Alone: Object and Fetishism," was published in **Books As Art**, *an exhibition catalogue published by the Boca Raton Museum of Art, Boca Raton, Florida, in 1991.*

[1] Stéphane Mallarmé, "The Book: A Spiritual Instrument," *Stéphane Mallarmé: Selected Poetry and Prose*, edited by Mary Ann Caws, (New York: New Directions) 1982: 83.

[2] Grubar, Susan, "'The Blank Page' and Female Creativity," *Critical Inquiry*, Vol. 7, no. 2 (Winter 1981): 246.

[3] Roland Barthes, "from The Pleasure of the Text," in *A Barthes Reader*, edited by Susan Sontag, (New York: Hill and Wang) 1982: 410.

[4] Susan Stewart, *On Longing*, (Baltimore, MD: Johns Hopkins University Press) 1984: 145.

[5] Ibid., 164.

[6] Pierre Cabanne, *Dialogues with Marcel Duchamp*, (New York: Viking) 1971: 61. Cited in *Marcel Duchamp* (exh. cat.), edited by Anne d'Harnoncourt and Kynaston McShine, (New York: Museum of Modern Art) 1973: 288-289.

[7] Benjamin H.D. Buchloh, "Marcel Broodthaers: Allegories of the Avant Garde," *Artforum*, Vol. XVIII, no. 9 (May 1980): 55.

[8] Dieter Schwarz, "Look! Books in Plaster!" *October* #42 (Fall 1987): 60.

[9] Irmeline Lebeer, "Dix mille francs de recompense," in *Marcel Broodthaers: Catalogue/Catalogus*, (Brussels, Palais des Beaux Arts) 1974: 66. Translated by Benjamin H.D. Buchloh in "Marcel Broodthaers: Allegories of the Avant Garde": 55.

[10] Clive Phillpot, "The success and failure of artists' books: an internal memorandum," unpublished notes for an address at the Artists' Books Conference, Boston University, 1985.

Buzz Spector: an interview with Neva Lindburg Muñoz

Neva Muñoz: Your work has been a series of unique objects, sculptures, collages. What is your interest in multiples?

Buzz Spector: Most of the materials I work with are taken from categories of things that exist in multiple. So I work with books, I work with postcards, and with photographs. Each book that I alter is part of an edition, part of the total population of copies of that book in print. I depend on the viewer's recognition of the futility of my destructiveness. When I alter a book, of course I destroy it as a text, but in the service of a transformation of one kind of value into another. I never intend for the alteration of an individual copy of a book to annihilate that book.

NM: What sort of books do you work with? BS: One of my most important works with an individual book might be the alteration of a copy of Harold Rosenberg's *Art on the Edge*. I was a student of Rosenberg's at the University of Chicago in the mid-1970s, and as a participant in his graduate seminar, "Art and Ideas," I guess I was one of his favorite people to argue with. At the end of the academic quarter he made a present to me of an autographed copy of his latest book. It turned out that that was the last class he taught; he died the next summer. Many people who were very supportive of my book altering activities were shocked when I tore pages out of the autographed Rosenberg book. And yet all I did was reduce by one the total number of copies of *Art on the Edge* in the world. What made it singular was that autograph, which was on the only page I left intact. By removing the text underneath Rosenberg's autograph, I wasn't editing his work. After all, what Rosenberg really produced was not that volume, but a handwritten manuscript that was submitted to a long publication process in which many people intervened to publish a multiple edition of his words.

NM: So how do you see your multiples functioning within the framework of the unique book object? BS: I like working with multiples because the art can be in more places than one. It can be distributed. It can be circulated. The sizes of the editions I produce range from three to 10,000, depending on the circumstances for exhibit. Remember, my book multiples cover two different categories: there are the photo-offset artists' books I've done in editions of a thousand, like *The Position of the Author*, and limited edition bookworks, much more materially invested, like *Silence: a synopsis* or the altered Marcel Broodthaers catalogue, in which I painted all the pages with gesso before tearing them out. These books operate midway between a purely mechanical edition and a purely crafted, unique object. Especially with the Broodthaers, each of the ten is categorically the same but specifically different, right? Even though the pages are all painted over with gesso, there are different brush marks on each page. Each of the torn pages is slightly different, too, although the process is the same. So you have, in my declaration of these ten books as an edition, a kind of challenge of the limits of the mechanical similarity that most preconceptions about editioning are based on. But we find in looking at more traditional, editioned fine print bookworks, the minor idiosyncracies that show up in an individual volume often make it more valuable to collectors.

NM: Do you look at the multiples in terms of Walter Benjamin's theory of the aura? Do you make multiples or editions to reach a larger audience? BS: Well, I don't flatter myself that an edition of ten becomes a mechanical exercise. Benjamin's challenge was to a notion of immanence that had characterized the value we place on art objects. In a world in which we know everything by its simulation first, what shock of aesthetic grace is left for the object to possess? I don't happen to agree with Benjamin's analysis. I think we find, over and over again, that the unexpectedness of great art is sustained despite our familiarity with its semblance in other materials, in other scales, and in other formats.

NM: **It looks like the edition of ten Broodthaers catalogues was made up of similar, but not identical, alterations.** BS: I'm interested in a working process that's, well, fundamentally obsessive. The tearing of pages that often characterizes my work is very liable to be read as obsessive-compulsive behavior. When I run the process through a defining context, the production of an edition, I don't entirely mask that aspect of the work. I think that if this kind of work is to be effective, it is in raising the issue of the compulsive behavior in relation to the disguises of marketing and distribution.

NM: **What about another feature of that obsessive-compulsive behavior? I am thinking of the tearing of pages in terms of repetitive motions which are often ascribed to the tasks of women. There are feminine qualities in that activity, both in the care and in the patience. Do you think that your work is feminized in a certain way?** BS: I think that many aspects of my work are feminine without making the claim that there's overtly feminist politics in my art. Not the least of the physical circumstances of my work are the opened page spreads I often use. The opened body of the book is, after all, twin white curvatures with a cleft between them. There's an erotic simile present, although usually unacknowledged, in looking at bookworks. And I think the things I do with books make that resemblance more overt—underscored, in fact, intellectually. Other aspects of my work—its repetitiveness, its small scale—associate themselves with various practices we call "women's work." But when you look at an artist like Ann Hamilton, say, who takes the notion of women's work and exaggerates it into gargantuan environments, we find that out of the simple, meticulous, engaged behaviors we call women's work, something immense and all-encompassing can arise. I try to make work that has a density of effect so that, even if the scale is small, the saturation of workmanship and visual effect is very rich. So that the person who looks at my work, holds it, scans it, can continue to be stimulated and engaged, somewhat in the way that any author stimulates and engages his readers.

NM: Touch on this aspect of desire, which I find to be a luxurious sort of wanting. Is the desire in your books just between reader and object, or do you find that the books stand in for another, a lover? BS: I think that the books are stand-ins, although I don't know that I want to psychoanalyze myself in this context. One thing I believe operates for people who view and handle my work is that they can readily empathize with the tactile aspects of my alterations. I think we all have a special kind of pleasure that we take, not from the recognition of a narrative or the appreciation of a motif, but from the brute materiality of any art object and the way it has been affected by a touch of hand. I think that, in the way that any reader turns the pages of any book, we can find something like a caress, a passage of hand as well as a passage of text. And in my sort-of-destructive altering of the book, there's still a touch of hand. I find often, in situations where readers can touch the altered books, they will touch them, they'll run their fingers across them and examine individual pages. It's a way of getting to know the work. Usually we can't touch art works. And, unfortunately, I find when my works move into institutional collections, they can no longer be touched. So part of the effect of the work is compromised. This is a problem I have with exhibitions of artists' books. Almost all of them, whether we're talking about unique sculptural objects or fine press editions, depend for part of their meaning on physical, temporal engagement by viewers. Locked in a cabinet, a book is absolutely mute, although its visage is still present. For me there's not a great deal of difference between looking at a book in a glass display case and looking at a very nice photograph of it in an art magazine.

NM: With your books, too, it seems the element of touch is a vital aspect of the work. If not the viewer's own physical contact with the work, then your initial touch, your mediation with the body of the book. BS: We find in a lot of feminist criticism of the relationship between reading and identity, a use of language which is almost a word play on rituals of courtship and the protocols of reading. Other artists do make the feminine aspects of the practice a politi-cal issue. I think of Mike Kelley, for example, and the stuffed animals and felt banners that he makes, all of which you might associate with ladies at church socials. But his work parodies the sincerity and devotional aspects of that context. I don't know that my work is in any way a parody of women's work. Moreover, I don't think it identifies itself in relationship to that idea. But sup-plementally, it certainly involves a model of making which, I hope, has none of the aggrandizement and rhetorical expansiveness that characterizes traditional male models of artmaking.

NM: I see your contact with books to be the same as the sensitivity of knowledge found in Roland Barthes' *A Lover's Discourse*. His voice is sincerely that of someone who is not in a controlling, "male," posi-tion. He speaks in the realm traditionally reserved for women, his stories are of desire, filling time, waiting. BS: I think the work is more about a kind of longing that you alluded to earlier. For one thing, in the books I alter, I'm removing material, so there's lost text. There's a narrative whose margins or whose middle is lost—

which could partially be reconstructed by a careful reading of what remains in the book, but never completely. In that way, I think the books I make operate as metaphors of memory. We always lose something, recollection is always partial. And even in the blank books I make—you know, *Silence: a synopsis* includes a blank book—you could see a metaphor of memory. Although in that book, I like to think of it more in relationship to the future than the past, because another way of regarding a blank page is that it hasn't been filled up with circumstances yet.

NM: So there are two interpretations. Instead of a book telling you its story, you have to write in your own... BS: Yeah. And in the *Silence* book, of course, there is another object, a cast glass human tongue. You can look at a severed tongue as a kind of complete silence, but there's nothing bloody about a frosted glass tongue. To me it's about speech that is in the act of taking form, not the silence of a physical mutilation.

NM: The tongue in the open book also becomes an erotic reference. BS: There's a lick of that, yes.

NM: Have you had any different interpretations of the tongue object in the piece? BS: Well, I remember when I showed the book to Renée Riese Hubert, the author of *Surrealism and the Book*, she picked up the tongue and handled it for a moment and then turned to me and said, "You know, this is very naughty." And I think that that's okay. The most socially sanctioned space for naughtiness we have is in the pages of a book.

NM: In the *Books as Objects* catalogue there's a quote from Lewis Barth about *Silence: a synopsis*. I couldn't tell which came first, the book or the quote. BS: That's a good relationship, then, between an object and a language. Lewis Barth is a rabbi and a theologian. He saw a copy of my book at his friends' house, friends also of mine. He had been feeling depressed about turning 50, and after seeing the open book on the table while conversing with those friends, he had a vision of it as a metaphor of the future. The future in everybody's life is the blank remaining pages of the book of their life waiting to have a story written in them.

A shorter version of this interview appeared in **Contemporary Impressions**, *Volume 2, no. 1, January 1994.*

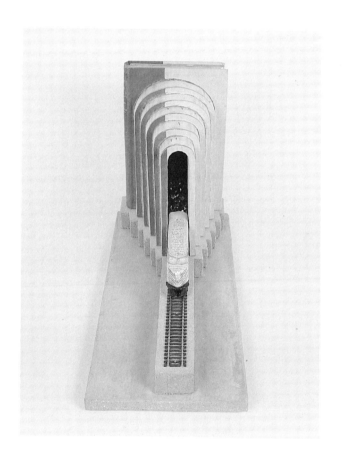

Margaret Wharton, *Tunnel Vision*, 1987
photo: William Bengtsen

Chambered Volumes:
The book constructions of Margaret Wharton

Margaret Wharton's art of the past 12 years is preeminently associated with the motif of the chair. One particular chair supported a heavier burden than any other in Wharton's 1981 solo exhibition at Chicago's Museum of Contemporary Art. A slice of a chair in profile appeared to emerge from each side of one of the main gallery's support columns. Stacks of similarly sliced books rose from each chair seat, ascending until they reached the ceiling. The work, entitled *Bookcolumn*, 1981, was a most astute illustration of the idea of the gallery space, suggesting itself as a structural element while being hung from the column it purported to support. There have been very few more successful elucidations of the uneasy relationship between the art object and the valorizing context of the museum.

Bookcolumn was one of Wharton's earliest works using books, but recently she has made a series of permutations of the book form. Utilizing found books, Wharton creates objects that retain some of the meaning and character of the original texts. The artist's strategies of disassembly and reconstruction are reminiscent of those employed in her chair works, but the eloquent titular wordplay of Wharton's book pieces resonates with the already present titles of her source objects.

The object made from a book has a long history. In addition to his boxes, Joseph Cornell made a number of book constructions dating back to the 40s. Among these, *Object*, 1940, featured a small round chamber carved out of pages of text within which Cornell placed a metal spiral, most likely a watch spring, behind a "window" of painted glass. However, Cornell's book objects were usually less eviscerated than adorned, serving as symbols of arcane knowledge.

In many cases, Wharton excavates the text body of a book, making a kind of chamber or box. Within this little room she reinstalls portions of the excised pages, carved and painted to resemble its furnishings. In *Poet's Flight*, 1987, a bulky anthology of contemporary poetry has been so eviscerated. The middles of its several hundreds of pages have been removed, their outer edges remaining as a roof and sides to an interior space. Sections of the book's front and back covers have been cut out, making windows through which a flight of stairs carved out of pages ascends toward a corner of the spine. The book has been exhibited on a cast concrete base resembling stairs, but it doesn't need the reiteration of this device to communicate its exquisite evocation of poetry's own spiritual ascent through the paring away of inessential language.

Reader's Digest, 1987, also possesses an inner space, but across the threshold cut through the front cover of this volume of "Condensed Books" is a bulging stomach of pages, complete with an esophagus that rises to the top of the interior chamber. The pun here is a broad one, comically literalizing the editorial condensation of several novels into thoroughly excerpted pap. A similar sense of satire invests *Fast Food*, 1987. The front cover of Shakespeare's *Romeo and Juliet* has been cut away to reveal a "Cliff's Notes" version of the play nestled within a frame of cut pages. Behind the humor there is a somber allusion to the death of intelligent reading, aided in part by the growing popularity of such shortcuts of comprehension.

A copy of a psychology textbook originally entitled *Psychoanalytic Interpretations* has had a number of successively smaller "arches" cut through it. These arches are mounted in front of each other, forming a tunnel shape from which a carved paper train emerges, atop a toy railroad track. On the intact rear cover of the volume a peephole has been installed, through which one can spy on the train leaving its bookish dark. References to voyeurism, sexual symbols—both phallic and vaginal—and an homage to Magritte compete for our attention. The work's title, *Tunnel Vision*, 1987, suggests a critique of the psychoanalyst's preoccupation with sexuality.

Symbols of another type appear within the space of Wharton's excised version of The *Joy of Cooking*, 1987. Pages carved into miniature atomic cooling towers float in front of the blue end paper of the volume's back cover, printed with the book's title in decorative rows. The effect is both sinister and serene, with the allusion to Three Mile Island's portentous near-meltdown balanced against the work's peaceful cerulean atmosphere.

The processes through which Wharton's bookworks come into being simultaneously mark the destruction of the original volumes. Unlike her transmuted chairs, the artist's altered books possess an extra poignancy derived from their effacement of an author's text. The viewer's realization that only one copy of a given work has been destroyed doesn't completely ease the disquiet evoked by that destroyed text.

Wharton's volumes have yielded up their textual narratives, but the space made through the removal of their pages is charged with new significance. These chambers hold the accoutrements of another order of telling. They are furnished with visions and dreams.

First published in **Dialogue**, *November/December 1987, Volume 10, no. 6, "Art Books" Column.*

The Tome, The Tomb;
On Broodthaers

The publication of a special issue of *October* (#42, Fall 1987), devoted to the writings and works of Marcel Broodthaers, and the announcement of Broodthaers' first major U.S. museum retrospective, to be held at the Walker Art Center, April-June 1989, has drawn new attention to the art and ideas of the enigmatic Belgian artist, who died in 1976. Broodthaers created a body of work distinguished by its radical aestheticism, eclectic materiality, and prescient reflectivity on the commodification of the art object. Central to his oeuvre are the many books and multiples he published. Broodthaers had been a poet and essayist before turning to the visual arts in 1964, at the age of forty, and a fragile and marvelous poetry infuses the objects he issued during the remaining twelve years of his life.

Poetry has little to recommend it in terms of economic sustenance, so Broodthaers pursued a variety of occupations. He worked for a while in a bank, and as a dealer in rare books. He also gave guided tours in the art museums of Brussels. Broodthaers had a number of friends who were visual artists, who declared Broodthaers to be an authentic "work of art" in 1962. Earlier, in 1957, Broodthaers had made his first film, *La clef de l'horloge*, a cinematic homage to Kurt Schwitters, and had subsequently taken up photography. Still, his exhibition at the Galerie St. Laurent, Brussels, marked the first public display of Broodthaers' artwork. The gallery announcement read as follows:

"I, too, wondered whether I could not sell something and succeed in life. For some time I had been no good at anything. I am forty years old... Finally the idea of inventing something insincere crossed my mind and I set to work straightaway. At the end of three months I showed what I had produced to Philippe Edouard Toussaint, the owner of the Galerie St. Laurent. 'But it is art,' he said, 'and I will willingly exhibit all of it.' 'Agreed,' I replied. If I sell something, he takes 30%. It seems these are the usual conditions, some galleries take 75%. What is it? In fact it is objects."

Among the objects of Broodthaers' first exhibit was a sculpture he made by imbedding the remaining copies of his last volume of poetry, *Pense Bête* (Think Stupid/Animal), in a base of wet plaster. The books, and a plastic ball, emerge from their plaster pedestal as a kind of memorial marking the internment of Broodthaers' career as a poet. Thus entombed, the books are worthless as texts, while being made simultaneously valuable in their new role as art. The ball, too, becomes an *objet d'art*, signifying perhaps in its encapsulated air the stilled breath of spoken poetry.

Broodthaers' subsequent publications elaborated on the transformation of language into object, taking the form of books, plastic signs, labels, and even the stationery of an imaginary Museum of Modern Art, whose various "departments" provided the theoretical framework for his large scale installations. The transformative process, however, was also one of cancellation. In 1969, Broodthaers published an altered version of Stéphane Mallarmé's book length poem, *Un coup de dés jamais n'abolira le hasard* (A throw of the dice never will annul chance), in which every word of the original poem was replaced (covered) by black lines of a length and height equal to the size of its several typefaces. Unreadable, the graphic array of bands still corresponds to the dimensions of the obscured text. *Un coup de dés* appeared in an edition of ten copies printed on anodized aluminum plaques, ninety copies of a 32-page book printed on translucent paper, and 300 "catalogue" copies printed on opaque paper. A fascinating aspect of the translucent version is its demonstration of the spatialization of language employed by Mallarmé. As the pages of this book are turned, the shadows of words to come and words passed can be seen through the sheets.

Broodthaers created a number of installations on the theme of the museum, revealing the uneasy relationship between the institution's cultural and economic functions. The first appearance of his work in the Midwest, *Un jardin d'hiver* (A Winter Garden), part of the 1977 "Europe in the Seventies" exhibition at the Art Institute of Chicago, was a recreation of the installation of the same name Broodthaers had assembled for a 1974 exhibition at the Palais des Beaux Arts in Brussels. Its nostalgic arrangement of folding chairs, potted palms, and framed or encased 19th-century engravings, was subverted by the television set in one corner of the room, surmounted by the observant eye of a video camera. The viewer staring at the set saw himself on its screen, acting the role of "museumgoer." The quasicatalogue Broodthaers published to accompany the installation combines reproductions of 19th-century engravings of rare birds and animals with pages of typographic samples of the kind found in printers' manuals. This bestiary proposed the alphabet itself as a collection of exotic species, and hints at the potential subversion of social and political references that accompanies acquisition of the artwork by the museum.

Broodthaers's last book epitomizes the delicate melancholy of his worldview. Entitled *La conquête de l'espace* (The conquest of space), 1975, it is described as an "atlas for the use of artists and the military." Measuring only 1" x 1", it contains silhouetted territorial maps of countries, reproduced as if they were all the same size. Its miniature scale is a precise cancellation of political space, and an ironic reminder of the distinction between art's aesthetic "territory" and the stereotypical national characteristics under which so many artists are now marketed.

*First published in **Dialogue**, May/June 1988, Volume 11, no. 3, in "Art Books" Column.*

The Departure of the Argonaut
The Museum of Modern Art

Composer, novelist, playwright, and painter, Alberto Savinio was a
career dilettante traveling the byways of Modernism. Born Andrea
de Chirico in 1891 (the younger brother of Giorgio de Chirico),
he was among the founders of the Metaphysical school of painting. He wrote his first opera, *Carmela*, at the age of 17, and four
years later appeared in Apollinaire's revue *Les Soirées de Paris*.
Hermaphrodito, his compendium of stories, poems, and theater
pieces, was published in 1918. Savinio continued to write, paint,
and design for the stage until his death in 1952.

"The Departure of the Argonaut" constitutes the final section
of *Hermaphrodito* (it is also the longest and most clearly autobiographical section). It appears here both as a *livre de luxe* published
by Petersburg Press, with English translation by George Scrivani,
and as an installation of unbound two-page spreads. (A trade edition in reduced size has also been published). Francesco Clemente
(who coincidentally was born the same year Savinio died) embell-
ishes the work with his graphic inventions.

Savinio's story is ostensibly concerned with the author's
induction into the Italian army and his subsequent departure for
the Salonika front in 1917. Savinio's textual journey transcends
time and space, his weirdly delicate and elliptical prose making
reference to such diverse characters as Dante Alighieri, Edgar
Allan Poe's Arthur Gordon Pym, Alex Godillot (inventor of the
life-jacket), the Three Fates, and Don Quixote. The writing
exudes a fascination with the colorful marginalia of existence.
Every object, hour, taste, and aroma is treated with exquisite, if
brief, attention.

Clemente's wildly diverse interests, wedded to his substantial inventory of drafting techniques, makes him a most appropriate visual interpreter of Savinio's masterwork. He approaches each of the book's five chapters, plus an epilogue, differently, exploring, among other things, the capabilities of lithography and the structure of the book form. The result is an extraordinary counterpoint of pictorial and linguistic fancies.

One spread in the first chapter features Savinio's notes about soldiers who must endure the tedium of train travel; it is overlayed by a looping platoon of male figures in ancient Roman garb. Minus legs and one arm, each gestures with his remaining limb, upward-pointing fingers touching the next torso in the arrangement. The military inferences, of martial mutilation and parade formation, engage the story at several levels. Clemente addresses the convoluted narrative in chapter 2 with a series of bizarre sailor's knots, tying the halves of each spread together across the gutter. Little boxes float beneath the type column on all but one right-hand page of this chapter. These containers hold a variety of hieroglyphlike symbols bearing no direct relation to Savinio's text, adding another layer of mystery.

The large-size of the book—each page measures 26 by 39 inches—provides Clemente with an ample working field. The lovers in the fourth chapter gambol upon great washes of color, the gutter here assuming an overtly sexual reference. Turning these pages becomes like pulling back the covers from a bawdy bed. The sumptuous, folded Japanese kozo paper sheets have the supple feel of bedclothes as well. Indeed, "The Departure of the Argonaut" functions as a kind of paginated seduction chamber within which the reader is aroused by color, texture, the heft and density of materials, as well as by the perambulations of its words and images.

*First published in **Artforum**, Vol. XXV, no. 6, February 1987.*

Anselm Kiefer's Bookworks

Books have been an essential component of Anselm Kiefer's art for more than twenty years, and an air of bookishness infuses the paintings, drawings, prints and sculptures that make up the rest of his prolific output. A number of Kiefer's most compelling large-scale images were first given form in the pages of his handmade volumes, while other books, paginated, but not meant to be read, stand among his most vivid artistic metaphors.

Perhaps the most striking evidence of the primacy Kiefer has given the book form was the artist's decision to reproduce one of his bookworks, *Durchzug durch das Rote Meer* (Passage through the Red Sea), 1986-87, at the beginning of the catalogue to his 1987 traveling retrospective organized by the Philadelphia Museum of Art and the Art Institute of Chicago. Preceding even the title page, this insert utilized extremely fine screen black-on-gray duotones and silver foil embossing to convey the chromatic and material effects of the original unique work. Ironically, the apparatus of the best quality offset printing was used to recreate the casual production values of Kiefer's own book, seventeen double page spreads of full-frame photoenlargements crudely pasted over boards stained, wrinkled, and occasionally splattered with strips of liquid silver. Kiefer's elaborate verbal-visual meditation on "passage" initiated the document assessing his work, inferring that first and foremost, his is an art meant to be read.

Indeed, Kiefer's design of the installation for the exhibition's inaugural venue at the Art Institute of Chicago put all of his bookworks into the first of its three large galleries. Visitors encountered eighteen of these objects, culminating in the sculptural tableau

Anselm Kiefer, *Breaking of the Vessels*, 1990
photo: St. Louis Art Museum

entitled *Ausbrennen des Landkreises Buchen* (Cauterization of the
Rural District of Buchen), 1975. This work consists of eight
opened books made from burlap covered with a greasy black
residue of burnt oil paint, charcoal, and glue. The books were
arranged in rows of four on a pair of white plastic laminated tables.

Mark Rosenthal has noted that these volumes are made from cut-up and burnt sections of Kiefer's own paintings: "This act of aggression on his earlier art produced a clean slate on which the artist could, in principle, state a revised vision of painting." The processes through which these books were made become an enactment of the ecological catastrophe referred to in the title. Buchen, the district where Kiefer's studio was then located, is also the site of a military fuel storage depot, and *Ausbrennen des Landkreises Buchen* reverberates between symbolic references to the ritualistic purifications of the studio and the (hypothetical) immolation of an entire region. In the Art Institute installation the two tables, flanking the central aisle, became a kind of scorched landscape through which one passed in order to reach the second gallery.

The scale of Kiefer's bookworks is relatively monumental; they are larger than most books in much the same way that his paintings are larger than most other paintings. The rhetorical grandeur of Kiefer's volumes is complemented by the welded iron lecterns that are their most common means of display. John Russell has described them as being "as big as the chained Bibles of long ago," a reference that conveys their austere and sacramental attitude as well as their imposing size and weight. The materials from which Kiefer makes his books impose as well upon the awareness of his readers. Kiefer's books made from lead are too heavy to be browsed through at all, and the cardboard pages of his other volumes, stiffened both by the cords that sew them together and the glues, papers, and pigments with which they are coated, yield only reluctantly to the effort of page turning.

Kiefer's earliest bookworks were less elaborately produced, but already exemplified the major themes of his art. In *Die Uberschwemmung Heidelberg* (The Flooding of Heidelberg), 1969, the imaginary disaster of the title is not literally depicted in either of the two versions of the work. Instead, Kiefer intersperses full-page photographs of arrangements of objects in his studio with found images of Nazi sculpture and architecture. The middle of each book is a double gate-fold of two panoramic views of Heidelberg, taken from a castle high above the city, and each version concludes with pages of brown wrapping paper treated with black oil paint. The inundation Kiefer has proposed is as much that of a repugnant ideology as of a natural catastrophe, and the vantage of the centerfold recasts the title as a reference to the action of a wrathful god.

Besetzungen (Occupations), first produced as a unique work in 1969 before being published in the West German art journal, Interfunktionen (Cologne, #12), in 1975, effectively satirizes the horrific political and cultural preoccupations of the Third Reich by presenting mock documentation of military conquest as a form of collective tourism. Kiefer, right arm raised in a Nazi salute, poses at a series of European sites of historical occupations; not those of the Third Reich, but of the ancient Romans. The artist's posturing is deliberately ridiculous, set up by his isolation in the midst of scenic expanses of beaches, fields, and ruins. The book's only bystander, in the background of Kiefer's Sieg Heil at the Colosseum in Rome, is walking away from the artist, apparently indifferent to his gesture. The problematic allegorization of the Third Reich through the monuments of the Roman Empire can be read as an anti-fascist critique, but as Kiefer himself has noted, "there are no truths, only interpretations of history."

Much within the extensive bibliography on Kiefer's art stresses its engagement with German and European cultural heritage, as well as the artist's interests in music, mysticism, and political history. Kiefer's paintings and graphic work, so physically commanding in their great scale, have also been accused of containing too much empty rhetoric. But the formal characteristics of Kiefer's books; sequences of images that can't be seen all at once; the necessarily physical interaction of page turning by the reader/viewer, and the material degradation caused by that handling; resonate with the artist's interpretive themes. Many of Kiefer's paintings have been executed on top of photographs, vestiges of which are visible through his retinue of mediums. The several versions of Kiefer's *Märkischer Sand* each operate as image palimpsests on which Kiefer's gestures in various materials are writ large upon his landscape views. The forceful conjunction of earth as subject and medium also obscures the details in his images that might connect them to a specific place or time. *Märkischer Sand V* (March Sand V), 1977, literally crumbles as its pages of photographs covered with sand are turned, a physical effect quite in line with the meaning of its pictorial narrative. The sequence of twenty five double-page images of wheat fields and distant horizons convey a sense of generic plenitude. These pictures, which alternate between details of stalks of grain and views of the distant hills and high horizon line, are at first only lightly streaked with grains of sand in dried glue. These smears become more extensive as each page is turned until, in the book's final spreads, the photographs are completely buried under layers of sand and gravel. *Märkischer Sand V* evokes time's annihilating passage in visual terms reminiscent of the abandoned ruins in the concluding lines of Percy Bysshe Shelley's poem, "Ozymandias": Round the decay of that colossal wreck, boundless and bare/ the lone and level sands stretch far away.

The archeological resonances of *Märkischer Sand* are premonitions of the conceptual and physical expansion of Kiefer's work in the 1980s. While still concerned with German cultural archetypes, Kiefer has expanded his references to include Old Testament episodes such as the Exodus, ancient Egyptian mythology, and the traditions of alchemy.

The title of *Kyffhäuser*, 1980-81, refers to the mountain under which, according to legend, the 12th century Holy Roman

Emperor Frederick I, also called Barbarossa, rests in eternal vigil, waiting to be summoned by the German people in time of need. Kiefer revises the legend here by transforming Barbarossa's magic sword into a winged palette, and in so doing establishes a punning relationship between the book's title and his own name.

The pictorial narrative in *Kyffhäuser* includes views of a dingy cellar "crypt," splashily overpainted scenes of a snowy forest floor, blurred photographs of a small fire eerily burning in the middle of a pool of water, and a number of found and rephotographed images, including a World War II scene of burning military trucks, views of the Barbarossa monument, and the stone head from a German memorial to the Unknown Soldier, whose caption Kiefer has altered to read, "the unknown painter." No story is clearly told in *Kyffhäuser*, but its multiplicity of graphic effects offers tantalizing avenues for reflection. Writing about a contemporaneous and similarly constructed bookwork, *Johannisnacht II* (Midsummer Night II), 1981, art historian Dorothea Dietrich noted how Kiefer's books "[do] not operate within one semiotic system, but use... two and, at times, three codes simultaneously: photography, painting, and handwriting." This clash of codes shatters their discrete integrity, forcing the viewer/reader to pick through the visual detritus of Kiefer's pages like an archeologist hunting for potsherds.

Shards are at the heart of one of Kiefer's most important books. *Die Geburt der Sonne* (The Birth of the Sun), 1987, combines references to the Pharaonic myth of Osiris and Isis with views of a Kiefer studio installation resembling the grid of fuel rods from a nuclear reactor. Kiefer's theme is creation and destruction: Osiris, the Egyptian god of the sun and also of the underworld; and the reactor core, whose manmade thermonuclear energy could also wreak terrible disaster.

Kiefer has mounted photographs on each of its nineteen

double-page spreads, although the images on the first nine spreads are mostly coated with reddish clay, to which is attached strands of copper wire glued to shards of white porcelain. These materials also festoon the surface of Kiefer's monumental painting *Osiris und Isis*, 1985-87, concerned with the same lesson: the search by the goddess Isis for the dismembered body of her brother and husband, Osiris.

In his catalogue notes on *Die Geburt der Sonne*, John Hallmark Neff describes the first half of the book as representing "aerial views of a 'desert'," and indeed the smeared and cracked dirt on these pages vividly evokes a parched landscape. Photographs of a desert landscape as well as of a Kiefer studio prop in the form of a jet airplane are visible beneath this surface. According to Neff, the "fragments of porcelain attached to copper wires, numbered and distributed in numerical order, one or two per page, represent the scattered pieces of Osiris."

The "nuclear reactor" photographs that make up the second half of the book are only lightly reworked. These dark, full-frame images have been embellished with thin lines of liquid silver that accent or supplement the copper wires connecting pieces of porcelain to the standing lead pipe "fuel rods" of the studio installation itself. Assembled in a concrete lined pit, the sequence of views shows this chamber being filled with water, an allusion both to the heavy water that insulates reactors and to the tears of Isis, whose weeping during the restoration of Osiris was said to cause the annual rising of the Nile.

In *Die Geburt der Sonne* Kiefer achieves an extraordinarily effective balance between image and medium. Paradoxically massive and frail, this volume mixes ideas of devastation and rebirth with material usages that transform the act of its reading into an excavation of cultural strata: turning the Earth's pages.

Baldessari's *Shandy*

Discombobulated from the moment of his conception, Tristram Shandy, the unfortunate hero of Laurence Sterne's 18th century epic, *The Life and Times of Tristram Shandy, Gentleman*, assays his circumstances through a multiplicitous discourse that collapses the conventional discretions of past and present, fiction and real life, and experience and memory. Through its narrator's constant interruptions, digressions, and reversals, Sterne expresses his own sense of the random, multifarious, and fragmentary quality of experience. Contributing to the general profusion of the book is Sterne's deliberate violation of typographic and signature conventions through strangely placed italics, capitalizations, asterisks, ellipses, and dashes; blank, black, and marbled pages; simulated legal documents, sermons, and passages in foreign languages; and chapters of wildly varying lengths. In its odd and often dazzling array of structural and narrative effects, *Tristram Shandy* prefigures such Modernists as Marcel Proust, James Joyce, and Virginia Woolf.

In 1988 Arion Press published a deluxe edition of *Tristram Shandy*, illustrated by John Baldessari. This three volume set includes an authoritative facsimile of Sterne's original text, bound in green calfskin and marbled paper over boards; a paperbound critical essay by Sterne scholar Melvyn New; and an accordion-fold book of Baldessari's photocollages, interspersed with Shandean quotations. The three publications share the same 6 $^3/_4$ by 10 $^1/_4$ inch format and are contained in a single slipcase.

Sterne measures up as one of literature's most ribald punsters. This country parson was a master baiter of lines to dangle before his voracious readers, exciting their prurient appetites through ironic redistributions and doublings of meaning. In a similar fashion, Baldessari's cropped and rearranged photoimages offer a visual rhetoric of sexual innuendo and deferred gratification, revealed through carefully executed compositional and installational strategies. While the wry Baldessari humor is an excellent complement to Sterne's affectionate bawdiness, the decision to publish these images under separate cover simply acknowledges that Tristram Shandy's typographic experimentalism makes it a book that illustrates itself.

Not that Baldessari's exercises aren't themselves enjoyable. His initial spread features two film stills, one above and the other on the left, facing some lines of text from the first chapter of Volume I, in which Mrs. Shandy's incautious interruption of her husband's act of engendering—"Pray my dear, quoth my mother, have you not forgot to wind up the clock?"—is blamed for the subsequent ruffling of young Tristram's "animal spirits." Both Baldessari images show male figures standing next to clocks, but while the faces of the timepieces are clearly visible, the faces of the men are obscured by circles of red (above) and green (beneath). The clock on the wall in the upper scene has no hands; its time is out. One of the three clocks seen in the bottom image is held up in the white-gloved hand of a tuxedoed figure. There is plenty of time here.

The pictures and accompanying excerpts are arranged sequentially, following Sterne's story line, such as it is. Baldessari's retinue of effacements and obscurations perform a service similar to that of Sterne's suggestive rows of asterisks, arousing libidinal interest through implications of moral censure. That these excisions have apparently been made on behalf of public morality is crucial to the understanding of Sterne's humor. As Samuel Taylor Coleridge once put it, "we have only to suppose society innocent, and then nine tenths of this sort of wit would be like a stone that falls in snow, making no sound because exciting no resistance."

Tristram's eccentric Uncle Toby, who is fond of riding a hobbyhorse, is one of Sterne's most amusing characters. Toby's extraordinary ingenuousness is manifested through his constant misunderstanding of statements and actions by others. He is the perpetual innocent before whom Sterne's wit is given form. Baldessari's still of a bathing beauty astride a toy horse is paired with a passage concerning the "communication" between rider and hobbyhorse, giving an erotic charge to Sterne's reflection on how the "heated parts of the rider... By long journies and much friction..." come to be filled with "Hobby Horsical matter." Any possibility of misreading these lines as expressing the pleasures of child's play is finally offset by the censorious blue circle covering the woman's face.

Baldessari's book is wonderfully well printed. The sumptuous matte paper gives the duotone black images a velvet glow. The overprinted colors are crisp and perfectly registered. The heft of the volume and the seamless flow of its accordion-fold text body join to convey a sense of graphic luxury. Against the lavishness of this presentation the kitschy thinness of the film stills is exaggerated; their indifferent quality as photographs per se is rendered all the more obvious. But this doesn't tell us something about Baldessari's source material we don't already know. The deliberately mediocre printing in such earlier Baldessari artists' books as *Brutus Killed Caesar*, 1976, or *Close Cropped Tales*, 1981, is all of a piece with the found images they contain. The exotic format here is also preceded, with variations, by the overlapping vertical and horizontal accordion-folds of *Fable*, 1977.

Baldessari has made an appealing homage to Sterne's lubricious yet sentimental world. His images maintain a hortatory distance from its antique convolutions, while the Shandean quotes invest his pictures with a subtle historicism. Like the Sterne volume it accompanies, Baldessari's *Shandy* is an admirable production; elegant in the hand and beautifully prepared for the bookshelf. But unlike Sterne's tale, which is also available in a number of inexpensive paperback editions, these photocollages are peculiarly rare. Was it so long ago that Baldessari wrote, "...since a lot of people can own the book, nobody owns it. Every artist should have a cheap line. It keeps art ordinary and away from being overblown"?

*First published, in slightly different form, in **Artforum**, Volume XXVII, no. 9, May 1989.*

Biblioselfconsciousness:
Walter Hamady's *Gabberjabs*

Printed, exquisitely, but cut, torn, folded, pasted, sewn, stamped, perforated, debossed, grommetted, taped, punched and bitten as well, Walter Hamady's Gabberjabs inventory the lover's discourse of the book maker, whose object of desire, spread before him, is receptive to every signature gesture. As readers of books, we are well aware of the erotic entreaties of which the text is capable. Roland Barthes identifies this desire thusly: "Writing is: the science of the various blisses of language, its Kama Sutra (this science has but one treatise: writing itself)."[1] Hamady's writing, in its lavish effulgence, offers many delights, but his wordplay is a lesser part of our engagement with his volumes than the textual experience Barthes had in mind. Rather, Hamady's book objects offer his authorial voice in, literally, dozens of material and procedural dialects. The visual and tactile charge of these pages bears the same relationship to the page spreads of conventional books that a bacchanale bears to phone sex.

In 1895, Stéphane Mallarmé noted how the wielding of the paperknife against the "virginal foldings" of the book"[2] was the claim to its possession. But the book of the nineteenth century was unaware of its hymeneal status. Its uncut signatures were simply a result of the bindery technology of the time. Still, the poet's penetrating observation helped instigate a revolution in the perception—and utilization of—the printed page. Mallarmé's recognition of the erotic aspect of cutting pages begins the critical consideration of reading itself as an activity of touch as well as mind. Touch, as enacted both in Hamady's construction of his books and in our readerly manipulations of them, is rewarded by a myriad of textures and tensions, resistances and yieldings, reminiscent of the grapplings of other passions.

Mallarmé's further reflections on the book as a common ground for the interplay of verbal and visual signs encouraged many subsequent textual experiments with the semantic potential of space, as well as furthering the development of the *livre d'artiste*. Hamady's own publishing house, The Perishable Press Limited, has produced several dozen *livres d'artiste* since its inception in 1964, including collaborations with artists such as Jack Beal, John Wilde, and Ellen Lanyon, and Paul Blackburn, Joel Oppenheimer, and Ann McGarrell, among many poets and writers. But it is in the nature of such collaborations to incorporate a certain tact, or restraint, whose abandonment is the essence of the Gabberjabs.

Steven Clay notes how the *Gabberjabs* "playfully yet assertively parody the structure, parts, histories and imagination of the book."[3] Parody is another word for burlesque, and it is perhaps in the latter term, with its sexualized and exhibitionist connotations, that Hamady's efforts are grounded. The *Gabberjabs* open endlessly to description. The itemization that begins this writing is itself only a partial listing of the ways in which Hamady has treated his materials. The stuff and substance of these books becomes another, exhausting, list. The writing itself, in its typographic variety, but more importantly, in its linguistic indiscretions, adopts the multitudinous cadences of seduction—imprecations, ejaculations, double entendres, baby talk, breathless extensions of sentences—to draw the reader ever more deeply into the situation. And the situation is one of apparently delirious excess. Like the dancer in a burlesque hall, however, Hamady's shakes and shimmers are quite deliberately choreographed. Rather than transports of unselfconscious bliss, his effects are enlisted in the service of an amorous projection: the book form as the body of the beloved.

It is Hamady's special brilliance to have found in the diminutive proportions of the book a kind of sensational amphitheatre, in which to expend his enormous energy. In *A Lover's Discourse*, Barthes praises this limitless (and amorous) expenditure as "exuberance...which is equal to Beauty."[4] Here is where Hamady's energy diverges from that of other bookish practitioners, for indeed, this exuberance has a melancholy aspect, coming not from a balance of desire and its gratification, but from a "disequilibrium...which marks [him] with its...intolerable luxury."[5] Within a genre practice too commonly afflicted with ingratiating preciosity, Hamady has found a way to give creative vent to a rage accompanying his longing. The crescent of teeth marks on a page of *Gabberjab* #6 is the most vivid emblem of the book maker's desire.

*First published in **Walter Hamady: Handmade Books, Collages and Sculptures**, an exhibition catalogue published by the Wustum Museum of Fine Arts, Racine, Wisconsin, in 1991.*

[1] Roland Barthes, from "The Pleasure of the Text," in *A Barthes Reader*, New York: Hill and Wang, 1982, 405.

[2] Stéphane Mallarmé, "The Book: a spiritual instrument," in Mary Ann Caws, ed., *Stéphane Mallarmé: Selected Poetry and Prose*, New York: New Directions, 1982, 83.

[3] Steven Clay, "Recycling Stuff by Starlight," in *Walter Hamady: Boxes and Collages* (exh. cat.), New York: Granary Books, 1990, n.p.

[4] Barthes, *A Lover's Discourse*, New York: Noonday Press, 1978, 85.

[5] Ibid.

Byron Clercx: Reading Things

We imagine that language is our tool, but it is we who are the tool and language is our master. —Paul Berman

You're all familiar with restaurant tools, those old saws, pickaxes, washboards, and other antique implements that are hung from the walls and/or ceilings of certain eating places to provide an ambience of honest labor. Rendered useless by breakage, wear, or subsequent advances in technology, these old things still stand for an ideal of hard work and hearty appetite. A casual glance at the gallery installation of Byron Clercx's *Power/Tools* might lead you to mistake them for more of such nostalgic decor. But look closer and you will see that a profound and subtle substitution has been made: what passes for woodgrain in the tool handles is actually an aggregate of laminated and carved book pages.

A similar substitution activates Clercx's "paintings." From a distance his series of wallmounted compositions of geometric elements read as paint on canvas, but scrutiny reveals them to be numbers of books mounted on wood panels and arranged so as to resemble the paintings of such Modernist masters as Piet Mondrian or Theo Van Doesburg. Indeed, the title of one such arrangement, *Piety*, 1993, is, in part, a pun on Mondrian's first name. Here Clercx has used a table saw to slice through some hardcover books, creating cross-sections of their texts, which he then places in rows upon a panel. The striations of typography made visible by this procedure look something like the pattern of wood grain on a parquet floor.

Piety doesn't look that much like a Mondrian, except to the degree that it uses a set of rectangular elements reminiscent of the art of De Stijl. But the physical texture and color of this work is only part of its meaning. Clercx's use of books evokes the complex arguments about meaning, interpretation, and transcendence behind the meager compositional syntax of the De Stijl artists. Its constituent texts, unreadable as they are in this circumstance, still signify textuality, operating, as Robert Scholes has noted in *Protocols of Reading*, in the provocative semantic terrain where the "figures of resemblance, contiguity, and causality" connect words and images. Another bookish work, *Theory*, 1993, is simply an arrangement of intact, closed clothbound volumes, sealed shut through applications of varnish, acrylic paint, and wood putty. Both authorship and subject are concealed from us by this means, although, theoretically, we could pull a given book from the array and read it in hopes of finding an explanation of Clercx's gesture. Of course, in so doing we would be destroying the art. Theory operates as an emblem of the unease we all sometimes feel in the face of contemporary art's more inscrutable manifestations. Who, on occasion, hasn't wished he or she had read the catalogue before encountering the work?

Clercx is well aware of the prophylactic agenda served by such reading, and offers us his *Untitled (Janson)*, 1991, a "crutch" made almost entirely from laminated book pages. When reading art historical or critical texts is used as protection against having to directly engage a subject work of art, then indeed such a book as H.W. Janson's *History of Art* becomes a kind of rhetorical crutch. In *Untitled (Form)*, 1993, Clercx has shredded a pile of self help manuals and religious tracts in order to make a cast paper chest protector like that worn by baseball catchers. Here is an object abounding in visual and material puns, ranging from the "fast pitch" of televangelists and therapy gurus through protection from the "hardball" aspects of life to our recollection that the catcher's equipment is referred to, in baseball parlance, as the "tools of ignorance." Baseball references also figure in *Big Stick*, 1993, a laminated text "bat," complete with a red velvet in wood carrying case. The texts Clercx employs are by Sigmund Freud, a choice that underscores, perhaps, the physiognomic reference all bats embody. Or it could be that the artist intended the object as an homage to one of the twentieth century's intellectual "heavy hitters."

But for the most part the metaphors of reading that Clercx employs are more generous, more amiable, and charged with a great love of the activity itself. The stitched latex book form of *Untitled (Respirator)*, 1993, is fitted with a hose and an air mask that can be worn by the viewer. As the person breathes into the mask the book form swells slightly with each exhalation, then contracts as the next breath is drawn. Thus Clercx establishes a symbolic connection between reading and living, between the book as an emblem of thought and breathing as emblematic of the flesh.

There is a diffuse nationalism in Clercx's inventory of objects. His various tools are simulated bits of Americana—read that doublehandled saw through the legend of Paul Bunyan, say, or the pitchfork in terms of Grant Wood's *American Gothic*—both mythically vague and emotionally loaded. Clercx's attention to his craft, too, evokes a distinctly American heritage of spare and graceful workmanship. All of his sculptures are made with a surplus of care that separates them from the internationalist anonymity of Duchampian Readymades or the appropriated consumer goods and antiquarian artifacts employed by such simulationist artists as Jeff Koons or Annette Lemieux. If Clercx's work lacks the critical acuity of simulationism, it is in part because the artist is less concerned with social commentary than with embodying a set of beliefs about the worth of things.

The experimentalism and variety of this work is also a reflection of the diversity of its maker's creative interests. Clercx loves the life of art in its social, historical, and philosophical contexts, and has produced a body of work whose material and conceptual generosity are shared with viewers in a most engaging way. He is, in short, a good read.

*First published in **Re/Formations**, the catalogue to an exhibition of Byron Clercx's work at the Sheehan Gallery, Whitman College, Walla Walla, Washington, November 9 – December 12, 1993.*

Residual Readings:
the altered books of Ann Hamilton

The gigantic and the minuscule coexist in Ann Hamilton's installations. The constructed environments that are the focus of
Hamilton's art involve temporary arrangements of objects, materials, and, often, human beings, in interior sites ranging in size from
several galleries of a museum down to a single room in a modest
house. So too does the scale of effects in her work range from the
heroic–its enormous accumulations of materials and labor–down
to the diminutive gestures of its human elements.

Hamilton refers to the people she includes in her installations
as "attendants" rather than "performers," and indeed the distinction is critical. Placed among the work's material and spatial
effects, these persons are meant to be seen rather than understood,
psychologically, and their absorption in their situation prevents us
from engaging them directly. The people in Hamilton's installations are indifferent to the physical proximity of viewers. We see
their stoic attitude in situations of confinement, exposure, or dis-
placement as a transcendence of personal circumstances while in
service to metaphors of the human condition.

In earlier works, Hamilton subjected her attendants to a variety of discomfiting confrontations with machines and materials,
but the artist now makes gentler use of them. Indeed, a casual
glance into several of Hamilton's recent projects would suggest
that their human resources were doing no more than writing in
the pages of printed books. Upon closer inspection, however, the
viewer discovers that "writing" to be one of several modes of era-
sure. First by literally rubbing off the words with gum erasers, and
subsequently by means of singeing or slicing them from the pages,

Hamilton has amassed a collection of books whose printed narratives have been completely effaced. But far from being silenced, these volumes speak instead of the mysterious labors of their transformation.

Hamilton began altering books in *indigo blue*, her 1991 installation for the Spoleto Festival in Charleston, South Carolina. Set in an old white brick garage that had previously housed several different industrial enterprises, the work was centered around an enormous (14,000 lbs.) heap of men's work pants and shirts, piled on a 17 x 24-foot steel platform. In the empty offices upstairs, many cloth sacks filled with soybeans were hung from the walls. As the beans sprouted, and rotted, during the course of the installation, the fetid smell of their transformation filled the air. The individual articles of clothing had all been washed, then folded and piled on the giant platform by Hamilton and her helpers. This devotional activity was itself a process of honoring the generations of anonymous industrial labor undertaken in the space.

Visitors who walked around the pile of clothing found a person seated at a wooden table, carefully erasing the pages from old military manuals containing the regulations for boundary jurisdictions. Working from the end of each book toward its beginning, a few words at a time were first moistened with a finger coated with saliva, then rubbed away with a Pink Pearl Eraser, until the volume was emptied of its text. Over the course of the installation a waste pile of rubber scraps and shreds of paper accumulated on the table, providing evidence of all the pages gone before this encounter. In this manner, four books were essentially scrubbed clean; their tattered pages comprising a space for the writing of another text, one acknowledging the labor that had facilitated the community's industrial and commercial past.

In 1992, Hamilton was commissioned to produce a limited edition of altered books, to be sold to benefit The New Museum of Contemporary Art in New York. The artist chose a total of fifty four volumes (40 in the edition, plus 14 artist' proofs) for the untitled project. These found books, mostly old novels or poetry, were selected for a variety of physical characteristics–size, wear, and paper quality–and for their typographic layout. Each book was opened to its middle, where six or eight pages were cut from the text block and reattached, edge-to-edge, to the right-hand side of the opened page spread, making an accordian-fold extension from the book. The eight pages thus displayed were meticulously rendered unreadable by Hamilton and several attendants who glued tiny stones over every word on the visible side. The finished books were then encased in shallow tabletop vitrines, made of black lacquered wood, whose width equaled the span of the artist's outstretched arms.

We can only imagine the intellectual exertions of the unknown authors who wrote those pages, but Hamilton's embellishment is concrete evidence of the labor expended in their obliteration. The neat rows of pebbles, nestled in blocks matching the proportions of the columns of text beneath them, comprise a minuscule terrain. It is as if an edifice of ancient language had crumbled under the force of centuries, leaving a granular residue that still corresponded to the structure of now vanished thought.

Hamilton's next book-altering project, *tropos*, was installed at the Dia Center for the Arts, New York, in October 1993. Entering the space, viewers walked on an enormous carpet of horse hair, stitched together from the tail hairs of hundreds of animals. Other alterations of the space were barely discernible, including the replacement of the clear window glass with translucent panes and the barely audible recording of a distorted voice emanating from behind the door to the freight elevator. In the middle of the space, a person was seated at a metal table, methodically singeing the pages of a book with a heated wire implement ordinarily used in wood working. As he or she passed the coil over the columns of type, a thin bluish plume of smoke curled upward from the disappearing words.

Here, as in her New Museum edition, Hamilton's selection of books was topically random, but materially and typographically specific. The hardcover volumes are of differing literary categories, but all consist of several hundred pages of solid text. The attendant moved the hot wire at the rate of slow reading, leaving visible the tops and bottoms of letterforms, like a kind of fringe for the column of blackened striations. Over the eight-plus months of the installation, 35 books were completely singed in this way.

The title of Hamilton's most recent installation with altered books, *lineament*, puns on her method of excision. Done at Ruth Bloom Gallery, Santa Monica, in the summer of 1994, the work took place in a room whose fifteen-foot high walls were completely covered with plywood sheeting. A rectangular plywood table was suspended on wires from the ceiling, and a plywood seat was similarly suspended near one end. Hamilton or one of her attendants sat there, partially concealed behind a small scrim mounted to the table, pulling long strips of previously cut pages from the text block of an opened book and rolling them into paper spheres. Once these balls reached an appropriate size–what "felt comfortable" in the artist's hand–they were pushed through the scrim to rest in the middle of the table.

For some two weeks prior to the opening the artist and several assistants had sliced the text blocks of several dozen books with X-Acto knives, cutting them so that each page of text could be pulled out, line-by-line, in a single strip. During the installation, these strips were wrapped together to make the balls. By the time *lineament* closed, thirty three such spheres rested on the table, each formed by the unraveling of a different text.

Here, as in all of the artist's previous book alterations, the longings of readership confront the voluptuous materiality of the books so transformed. The outermost strips of the paper balls are almost readable; their delicate textual and material variety is reminiscent of so many little globes. But the pleasure we take from this effect is complicated by the textual annihilation they confirm.

It is no recourse to console oneself that the books Hamilton alters aren't literary classics. To consider her methods in any proximity to writing is to misconstrue them as forms of criticism. Yet Hamilton's books are anything but wordless. Every page is marked with signs of the touch that effaced their texts. This touch, simultaneously obliterating and tender, reiterates qualities of hand seen elsewhere, and in much larger scale, in Hamilton's installations. Of all the residues of Hamilton's work, these volumes are the most poignant. They are gestural palimpsests, their various narratives covered over by procedures that concretize the behaviors of writing into the presentness of art.

Caprices

Jo Ann Callis, *Hair and Beets, 1976*
photo: Courtesy of the artist

Hair and Beets

The fragment of text that occasions this writing is from an essay I was commissioned to write about the photographs of Jo Ann Callis. It's a passage I particularly liked, but which doesn't appear in the published text, for reasons other than its disclosure of a particular erotic moment. I am offering it here less as a narration of an image's means than as a reflection upon the topography of desire.

In 1978 Callis made a silver gelatin print of a recumbent figure on a rumpled bed, next to whom had been placed a bunch of beets. Later that year she changed from black and white to color format work, a circumstance that left this image outside the trajectory of the artist's career, as recuperated by the institution commissioning my words. Sharing the world with all the artist's subsequent production, it became supererogatory through no fault of its own. Indeed, the problem of this work, its expressive purpose, is flawlessly constituted, joining form to medium in a way that shakes loose the potential marvelousness of both.

Here is what I wrote:
"The sunlight passing through an unseen, partly shuttered, window makes a pattern of shadows falling diagonally across wall, bed, and the bare, heavily freckled back of a young woman with long hair, lying on her side and facing away from the camera. From behind, it is virtually impossible to tell the sex of the subject, whose androgynous figure reclines in a position of sumptuous intimacy. Her hidden left arm is bent so that her head rests atop her forearm, the fingers of the left hand visible at the junction of neck and abundant dark curls. From amid the tresses that cascade along the top of her head protrude the roots and globular forms of a trio of beets.

"The beets are not easily seen. In the black and white photograph they are as dark as the hair within which they are nested. Even the sinuous extensions of their taproots, prickled with rootlets, resemble additional tendrils of the woman's hair. The illumination also cuts diagonally across the creases and folds in the glossy bedsheet, complicating the design of lights and darknesses that plays across the field of the image. The freckles on the woman's back seem a fleshly reiteration of this shadow play. Our search for those titular vegetables brings us close to that shining hair and the mysteries poised there, and the close tones of hair and beets conjures up a memory of the agreeable scents of shampoo and the freshly disturbed dirt from which the beets have been pulled."

I showed a draft of my essay containing this passage to the artist, who, in the course of checking the manuscript for errors of fact or other misrepresentations, noted that the subject in *Hair and Beets* was, in fact, male. I commented that my words about how "virtually impossible" it was to tell the sex of that reclining form were better chosen than I had realized. She laughed, and we moved on to other things.

As I examine the image again, I can see that its unresolvable androgyny is mostly a function of cropping and camera angle. Still, despite my textual acknowledgment of the strategic arrangement of the scene, I had assigned the figure a sex, and had chosen descriptive language according to that engenderment. The invitation to the viewer suggested through the relaxed abandonment of that supine form recalls Barthes' reflection on the capability of the erotic (photographic) image to launch desire beyond what we are permitted to see. The erotic charge of *Hair and Beets* resides in the amour of photographer and subject given form through nuances of pose and light. I saw that suggestion of bliss and named it according to my preference, but the excellence of the image is in how generously the artist shared the body of her desire.

*Published, in slightly different form, in **Caprice**, January 1989.*

A Letter to Anne Rorimer
about Marcel Broodthaers

Dear Anne,

I read of a triumphant preparation of mussels in Roy Andries de Groot's *Feasts for all Seasons.* The still living animals are cast into the sink under cold running water and the clumps of seaweed and accrustations of barnacles on their shells are scraped away with brushes and old oyster knives. Of course, you must discard any half-opened shells (most unpalatable) or any that are suspiciously heavy from internal sand. Then put them into a large bowl, covered with water, and salt to the taste of the sea. Having thus made them welcome, toss in several handfuls of flour. The mussels will regard this as a grand meal, and in a few minutes there will be a gentle stirring and scraping as they open up to dine. Set the bowl in the refrigerator, where the banquet continues all night, until the mussels have glutted themselves to a fat whiteness, at the same time voiding themselves of all dirt. In the morning the water is black, and when the mussels have once more been rinsed under cold running water they are ready themselves to be eaten.

Seeing the Broodthaers exhibition at the Museum of Contemporary Art in L.A. revived my taste for mussels, and for a number of other things. The last time we dined together, amid the palmy decor of that German restaurant near the Art Institute, Marcel was our subject. We missed a chance to consecrate him when we ordered the liver instead. His *livres d'artiste* occupied our talk, as I recall. Was it of *Pense Bête* that I proposed an "interred diction"? You explained that the rows of ink blocks traversing the pages of *Un coup de dés...image* followed exactly the placement and scale of the text of Mallarmé's poem of the same name. What a contradictory homage, I mused, to invoke the Symbolist poet by censoring his every word.

But ah, those mussels and eggs: in incongruous numbers, in pots or on panels, on chairs or tables. What shall we make of these? Michael Compton's catalogue essay proposes them as models of social molds. But in the quote he offers by Marcel, isn't another appetite inferred? "Four forms are necessary for me, mussel, egg, the pot which I already feel capable of filling. And the Heart..." Think about all those seventeenthcentury Dutch and Flemish tavern scenes, a little industry of immoral iconography, whose most relentless practitioners—Jan Steen and Hendrik Pot—serve us broken eggs and opened mussels as emblems of easy virtue, at the feet of laughing barmaids and drunken men. And here or there a lecher who smokes, poking his little finger into the bowl of the upraised pipe in his lap. We know that this is not a pipe.

I remember that Marcel worked as a dealer in antiquarian books, wherein such ribald depictions often appeared, and that he gave guided tours of the Palais des Beaux Arts in Brussels. Aren't a few such generic interiors mounted there? Marcel had a taste for living which was perhaps bawdier than his most solemn advocates might admit. His open letter on the inauguration of the Section XIXème Siècle in the first of his fictional Musée(s) d'Art Moderne included this passage: "The speeches were on the subject of the relationship between institutional and poetic violence. I cannot and will not discuss the details, the sighs, the high points, and the repetitions of these introductory discussions. I regret it." This congress sounds animated indeed.

Two of Marcel's *Decors* were included here. At the entrance of the exhibition was *L'Entree de l'exposition*, an entrancing garden of palms and figures. It concluded with *La salle blanche*, whose unvarnished lexicon provides the perfect image of his endeavor. In between, a voyage through a sea of residues, a fluent sign language.

Marcel was certainly a man of letters. We hang upon his every word. This potpourri of placards, postcards, and playthings is in no sense innocent. His work persists in its frail and melancholy grace, even in the case of this adulatory installation. Its refusal to be completed by being here, in such a retrospective, is its real achievement. As such, it leaves us hungry for... what? The mussels are the specialty of the house, but you'll have to taste them with a foreign tongue.

Informally yours,

*Previously published, in slightly different form, in **Art Issues**, no. 7, November 1989.*

Touching, Turning, and Yearning

I pause before one of my bookcases. Somewhere here, I muse, is a passage that will serve as an epigraph for this writing. This top shelf is for philosophy and lit-crit: Adorno through Gerald Graff. These subjects play themselves out two shelves below. I like ordering my library topically by shelf, alphabetically by author. This occasionally leads to uncanny juxtapositions: Jean Gagnon's *Pornography in the Urban World* next to William H. Gass's *On Being Blue*, for example. The biographies have a couple of shelves of their own, and on the bottom, the spillover, from the neighboring case, of the critical journals. Here is a row of *Critical Inquiry's* dour black spines, with volume and issue numbers in annual repetitions of yellow, red, blue, and green; The *New Criterion's* spectrum of pastels; and *October's* clinical white, title in black caps, issue numbers in red, except for the mistake their printer made with #41.

Moving to another case, I run my fingers along the shelves of art magazines. I feel a uniform slickness, hard, austere, cadenced by edges of issue after issue. With the exception of *Artforum*, none of the major art magazines have interesting looking spines. In a bookcase, nearly everything in the artworld is black on white. But the collective sheen of the glossy covers is rather sexy. These varnished objects are slick and supple when pulled from the shelf, lolling in hand or lap with a mixture of abandonment and aplomb.

In José Donoso's novel, *A House in the Country*, the immense library of the Ventura family, claimed to "encapsulate all human knowledge," is itself an elaborate fiction; its four stories of embossed gold on leather spines are exactly that, simulated backs of books, glued to the wall. An unfortunate reader, lured by the abundance of titles, pulled mightily at one such "volume" on an upper level before losing his grip and tumbling backwards through the railing to his death. I can understand the mortal ferocity of that tug, however. What book lover wouldn't want to reach into such a sumptuous array and pluck a morsel? And having plucked, to open the stiff husk to confront the pale and striated sustenance within?

Opening a book for the first time, you realize some important particulars about the means through which your readerly desires are to be gratified. I like reading smaller books on my back, head propped up by two pillows, each folded in half. I balance larger books against my upraised knees, but this is pleasant only if the text type is sufficiently large to be read across the resulting six extra inches of space. I value lightness in this position, as in the Harvard University Press hardcover edition of Italo Calvino's *Six Memos for the Next Millenium*, whose material discretion (creamy matte paper, emphatically legible typography, appropriate scale and heft) is utterly engaged with its discursive texture. Calvino's lightness goes with "precision and determination, not with vagueness and the haphazard." He cites Valery's admonition, "Il faut être leger comme l'oiseau, et non comme la plume' ('One should be light like a bird, and not like a feather')."

On the other hand, the Bompiani *Futurismo & Futurismi* catalogue is sheer morbid weight. From its gleaming aluminum-finish cover, through its 638 dull enamel pages, each measuring $11^{1}/_{2}$ by 8 inches, to its dense columns of 8 point type, everything about the volume conveys brute metal substance. Turning its pages is so likely to slice the reader's fingers that the book should be read with gloves. A friend of mine, who runs a used bookstore specializing in art publications, has attached a notice to his copy warning browsers to get a good grip on the catalogue lest it slip and break one of their feet. My pleasure in looking at its pictures is tempered by the constant minor effort involved in making the book stay open, and the major irritation at having to read it at a desk or table since its poundage on my chest is insufferable.

The topography of an open book is explicit in its erotic associations: sumptuous twin paper curves that meet in a recessed seam. In *Sade, Fourier, Loyola*, Roland Barthes yawned at Sade's enumeration of tortures, while admitting to a disturbance at the narration of sewing a victim's anus and vagina shut. Barthes characterizes this sewing as "the most spiteful of castrations, indeed, since it makes the body retrogress into the limbo of the sexless." The Sadean stitching suggests a body to be read, wholly abject. And this body, sealed off with red waxed thread, is like a book whose cut pages have been perversely mended in order to be sliced by a reader's knife again.

The reader's passage through a book is a repetitive activity, with a great many sweeping and attentive gazes leading to somewhat fewer turnings of pages. We call deluxe precisely those volumes that supplement mere cognition with a rhetoric of apprehension and handling. The whole book can only be known if we add the knowledge of the hand, ear, and nose to that of the eye. This is not a trivial point: a book that cannot comfortably be held; or which stinks of mildew; or whose pages crumble when turned, will be more difficult to read very well.

But I've forgotten my epigraph. Several books have passed through my hands in the course of typing this essay. Once I've finished my work I will return to one of them. Thoughtfully, I'll turn its pages. More words await me there, or maybe a picture. What a pleasure it will be.

Vertigo

There's a Chinese proverb to the effect that "things themselves are lying, and so are their images." Of late the idea of simplicity has returned. But things move so fast now that they have a tendency to become less pure. I yearn for those ornamental moments, such as a justified apology, or a taste that reveals both an appetite and the shape of its gratification. At a party some people I didn't know were playing a game in which each one in turn struck a pose and the others would guess the situation from which it came. Was it Kenneth Clark who said that you couldn't depict movement without distortion?

Longing seeks its object in the middle distance, in the zone beyond its grasp but before the horizon. Up close and personal we know what's going on. Far out it's all a shadow play. In between, things change, in the spaces we don't remember. Down the street a man is waiting for the light to change, adjusting his collar while gazing at the traffic. Eyes closed, a woman leans her head against the window in a passing car. He is reminded of Modigliani's reclining nude: erotic, indifferent, perfected. Haven't I seen you someplace before?

*Previously published in **Vertigo**, a book edited by Christian Leigh for Edition Thaddeus Ropac, Salzburg, Austria, 1990.*

Some Family Photographs

April 1966

The giant hot dog is clipped from the newspaper. I am standing in
my parents' bedroom, holding it up to my face, mouth open, as if
taking a bite. I am bare chested and my muscles are flexed, to document my recently accomplished physique, the result of several
months in the high school weight room. My mother and I were
arguing about Andy Warhol, and this photograph was intended, in
part, as a riposte to her complaint that Pop had nothing to do
with Art.

June 1973

My daughter, then four, is curled in a fetal position on the sidewalk
next to a fire hydrant; the bright splash of her body counterpointed
by its bulbous shadow. She is playing dead. It must be late morning, but although the sun is shining brightly, she is wearing a cable
knit sweater over her flowery dress. The night before I had called
the police after my wife and I awoke to the screams and thuds of
our downstairs neighbor beating up his girlfriend. We wondered if
the child had heard the noise. Seeing her sprawled on the pave-
ment we knew the answer.

November 1975

I am standing in the kitchen of my house in Durham, North
Carolina, dressed in a green plaid flannel shirt and tan work pants.
I'm holding a white coffee cup whose double finger holes identify

it as a souvenir from my days as editor of the college literary magazine. I wore my hair long at that time, and it has been combed out to make an Afro. I don't remember who took the photograph. Renting this place was a last ditch effort to keep the marriage together, but my wife had moved out anyway two months before. An open cabinet door shows a single dish.

September 1981

This is a picture from our wedding—her first, my last—in the studio we shared in Chicago. We held the ceremony across the hall, in our neighbor's relatively empty loft, then brought everyone over to our place for the luncheon. The photograph was taken from the raised platform where we slept, and it shows several tables of guests eating slices of wedding cake. I no longer remember the name of every person in the scene. Of course, the bookshelves along the far wall contained my entire library at that time, and I don't remember every title either.

December 1987

The Art Institute was organizing an exhibition of my work and had asked me to provide an image of myself for the catalogue. I wore a black turtleneck and tried out various expressions in front of the camera. My daughter came with me to the photographer's studio, and she laughed at my attempted seriousness. There were some shots left on the roll, so the photographer asked her to strike a pose. She offers a wry, closed mouth smile, with one eyebrow raised. Her forearms are crossed above and slightly behind the subtle tilt of her head. I am stunned by her beauty.

July 1988

Seven photographs of the Painted Desert, overlapping slightly to make a panorama. The car appears in the first image and my wife, wearing sunglasses, is seen in the last. In between is an arc of gravel, a bit of metal railing, and myriad little mounds of striated color. This is en route to California, and the real subject of the arrangement is the sequence in and of itself. Make no mistake about it, we're looking at expanded possibilities here.

August 1991

I stopped at the florist on my way home and bought laurel wreaths for the three of us. My wife and I took turns photographing each other, garlanded and holding the naked baby. There's a note of embarrassment in our smiles. We're only temporarily pagan. But our little boy is all radiant animal gladness. He leans into the soft hollow at the base of his mother's neck, claiming her before the camera's eye.

September 1994

My mother is seated at a grand piano. She is reading the music as she plays. The band of darkness on the left side of the image is a curtain. It merges with the black expanse of the instrument to frame her in the cone of light from the lamp mounted above her right shoulder. The side of her face, her upper arm emerging from the sleeve of her black dress, and the double strand of pearls, are the brightest moments of the image. She is twenty years old, but that look of concentration is one I recognize from all the rest of her life.

*First published in **Family Album**, the catalogue to a group exhibition curated by Betty Brown at the Main Art Gallery, Visual Arts Center, California State University, Fullerton, September 10 — October 9, 1994*

Biography

Buzz Spector is an artist and writer who has been involved in the book arts for more than twenty years. His work with the book as subject and object has been shown in such museums and galleries as the Art Institute of Chicago, Museum of Contemporary Art Chicago, Newport Harbor Art Museum, Corcoran Gallery of Art, and The Mattress Factory. Spector has issued a number of artists' books and editions since the mid-1970s, including, most recently, *The Position of the Author* (Visual Studies Workshop Press, 1993) and *A Passage* (Granary Books, 1994).

Spector was a co-founder of *WhiteWalls*, a magazine of writings by artists, in Chicago in 1978, and served as the publication's editor until 1987. Since then he has written extensively on topics in the book arts, among other aspects of contemporary art and culture, and has contributed reviews and essays to a number of publications, including *Artforum*, *Art Issues*, *Dialogue*, *Exposure*, *New Art Examiner*, and *Visions*. He is the author of numerous exhibition catalogue essays, including *Ann Hamilton: Sao Paulo—Seattle* (University of Washington Press, 1992), and *Jo Ann Callis: Objects of Reverie* (Des Moines Art Center, 1989).

Spector earned his B.A. in Art from Southern Illinois University at Carbondale in 1972, and his M.F.A. with the Committee on Art and Design at the University of Chicago in 1978. In 1991 he was awarded a Louis Comfort Tiffany Foundation Fellowship, and in 1982, 1985, and 1991 he received National Endowment for the Arts Fellowship Awards. He currently teaches at the University of Illinois at Urbana-Champaign, where he is professor in the School of Art and Design.